REMARKS OF UNCERTAIN CONSEQUENCE

'the conflation and confusion of aims and criteria
is the normal and original condition of mankind'

Ernst Gellner

Remarks of Uncertain Consequence

Alan Halsey

FIVE SEASONS PRESS

2022

Published by Five Seasons Press
41 Green Street, Hereford HR1 2QH UK
www.fiveseasonspress.com

ISBN 978-0-947960-99-5

Cover and tailpiece drawings from the author's
Self-Portraits for Removal from an Exhibition

Thanks to the editors of *Free Poetry*, *Past Simple*, *Split Level Texts*,
Stride, *Some Roast Poet*, *Route 57*, *Black Box Manifold*,
Golden Handcuffs Review and *Junction Box*
in which some of these pieces first appeared

Typeset in 12.5 on 15.5 Ehrhardt
at Five Seasons Press
and printed on
Five Seasons book quality recycled paper
by
Short Run Press Ltd
Exeter EX2 7LW

the element is as liminal does

———

On the summer solstice
2013 we were reliably told

there had been 'a big
revolution in transparency'

in other words a
funnel plot in which

'the less procedures
the wider the funnel'.

We were also told
that if we looked at

our arms we might
see lightning flowers.

———

a sea of wiseacres —
holy day of ambiguities —
it's for the commercy sake
of them that speak leasing
[Ps. 5:6]
we've been saved

('One reads
in order to ask questions' —
that's Kafka —
query the pronoun —
'lost among these
entirely strange people')

(((yea tho' I walk in the
shadow of the German
dentists in Lanzarote
I'll remember Zarathustra
& laugh & sing & fear no
categorical imperatives))

———

Arriving in Moscow December 1949
Mao Zedong was heard to remark
'I am here to do more than eat and shit.'

How wrong could Mao be not to guess
his boghouse was bugged. His shit collected
and analysed. End of Sino–Soviet pact

due to low levels of amino acid and
a lack of potassium which indicates
a nervous disposition. At least

that's what the BBC has to say.
Moscow made no comment and
developments were left for another day.

1 Jan 2016

Tentative at ten to two a.m.
just before death's cousin mass hysteria
shows up with a brochure entitled
'Extinction Coefficient'. I once started
to write a book of that name
but we can't always be going
back to the womb or can we?
It's less than a month since the first
Ginger Brit blasted off into space
and that was only shortly after
somebody told the *Daily Star* that
Giant Rats Ate Our Xmas — and
that was not so long after we heard
that vultures are killed in the belief
that ingesting their brains bestows
special powers with the comment
'This is very troubling for vultures.'
And now you're telling me
language is inadequate. Isn't
it not 'in-' but 'over-'?

———

[Amazulu shaman: my thanks.
The day after I read how you
found lost things by descending
into your own dark deeps
the desk drawer I'd fruitlessly
rummaged through time after
time has when I was searching
for another also lost thing un-
disappeared my purple notebook.
To continue:]

on heritage, for Laurie Duggan:

1. To come home from Worcester
that Faithful City & to find
No Particular Place to Go.

2. The centrepiece of Worcester Cathedral
is King John's tomb with the lion underfoot
munching the point of his sword.
That wicked King John. The Scottish
guide says 'What do you expect?
He was a king.' Overlooking, I think,
another and quite crucial point.

3. Geraldine tells me I missed
the memorial to the author of
Eikon Basilike — or one of them —
I mean the author, not the king.

4. It's said the future Charles II hid in
the cathedral tower to watch the state
of play that afternoon his Scotsmen
were taking an awful beating. This was
towards the end of the cricket season
then regarded as top battle time.

5. Visiting Worcester a century later
Messrs Jefferson & Adams were perplexed
that locals had heard of no such battle.
There were probably no Scots still in town.

6. I digress. I only meant to say
now I'm back up north: inside Yorkshire too
there's a small place called Wales.
It should not be mistaken for the unit
of measurement so frequently cited.

———

That a soul must have a soul
& the soul's soul a soul —
the living-dead souls of Egypt
in infinite regression —
before anyone looked at souls
pictured coming forth by day
& saw they were harpies —

What a loss to religion
when gods' buttocks
& underlings' refusal
to drink piss &
eat shit were no
longer considered
scriptural topics —

When snakes grew legs
When crocodiles could talk
When 'sky' meant the safest of places
& men become swallows
sported round the heads
of friendly golden baboons —

When an eggshell had two spirits
one to guard it before
& one after it was cracked
so that every eggshell was two eggshells

———

'Send him to Colney Hatch'
Voltaire's said to have said
about this or that theologian.
A good idea but Colney Hatch

didn't open as a madhouse
until the year of the Great
Exhibition. I've searched
and searched but have yet

to discover why Colney Hatch
had such a reputation
as to land this development.
I did find the photo captioned

'renovated building in use as
flats, 2008'. The watchtower
with cupola atop. Very
19th century, so post-Voltaire

but consider also that
'Care in the Community'
enabled this latest change
of use. Voltaire would

sit down on the verge
of the North Circular
and weep to think of so
many theologians let loose.

——

'Like a deal of old coves
that has nothing to do
but hidles away time
in reading or pottering
about a garden'

— do you see me? —

You're listening to the
sponge-merchant's tale
as Mayhew told it —

'I do believe people
reads theirselves silly,
he would
talk away stunning'

———

London smog in the 1950s
as a history video on youtube
isn't entirely the same as

but I do remember the knitted
balaclava with only holes for
eyes my mother must have made
& made me wear as we waited
at the Home & Co bus-stop
on Thornton Heath High Street
& we couldn't see the bus
until it was a few yards away

then I saw it was Uncle Doug
at the wheel Uncle Doug with his
undertaker's son's sly waxy grin
who when off duty slipped into
something more comfortable
& turned I was told into Auntie

Archival note. The author's papers show that he spent the lockdowns of 2020/21 pernicketing with this and other remarks of uncertain consequence. In earlier drafts he identified the bus-stop as 'outside Liptons', adding a footnote correctly asserting that Liptons is now mainly known for supplying lowgrade tea to tourist hotels. In those timeheavy months it seems he not only recalled the provenance of his Uncle Doug's grin but realised he'd conflated Liptons with the Home & Co aka the Home & Colonial Tea Association whose distinctively elongated typographic legend was a feature of Thornton Heath High Street during his childhood. Liptons had merged with the Home & Co in the 1920s, when the latter's chairman was the long-serving William

▷

Slaughter whose connection with the British colonies may simply be an accident of name. Nevertheless and seemingly embarrassed by its imperial suggestion the Home & Co traded after 1961 as Allied Supplies, as which it was acquired by the notoriously enterprising James Goldsmith. It subsequently merged with Safeway UK, now also as defunct as the British Empire which the Home & Co if only by title outlived. The 'knitted balaclava' appears in the earliest draft dated 2015, before face coverings became a feature of the author's later life as they were of his childhood.

———

Mrs White
had a fright
in the middle
of the night

which at 8 or 9
I thought meant
my schoolmate
Robert White's

mum who was
sent to Cane Hill
which last week
I saw again from

Farthing Down.
Or what remains
of it after partial
demolition and

a fire soon after.
That asylum tower
warning to us all
& now but not then

looking north
the Gherkin & its
giant neighbours.
The new city which

▷

is not Jerusalem.
Pale Robert in need
of a dinner & his
mum the divorcee

she saw a ghost
eating toast
halfway up
a lamppost

——

Have you seen the engine drivers' girls and boys
on a summer evening at Streatham Common station?

No but tell me where I'll see the engine drivers' girls and boys
this summer evening at Streatham Common station.

Look past the end of the platform and you'll see
the engine drivers' girls and boys. I looked and looked

that summer evening at Streatham Common station but
still I couldn't see the engine drivers' girls and boys.

Look really hard. Look harder. Yes yes they're playing
past the end of the platform this summer evening

lively motes of dust in tired eyes. Yes I've seen those sprites
mothers and fathers call the engine drivers' girls and boys.

(snapped & unsnapped: first notes on absence)

The thing about my late mother's photo collection is for me my frequent absence and it's not only that we didn't share much of my life after I'd as is said grown up for there are or were photos I distantly yet distinctly remember of the toddler me such as the sandcastle builder squatting spade in hand outside a holiday caravan in I think it was Broadstairs but anyway on the Kent coast and my father with Silvikrined hair unusually ruffled stood behind me ludicrously wielding a saucepan and grinning. I'm sure this photo was taken with our family's only and then popular Brownie box camera producing small square black or rather grey and white prints and to me it is as palpably missing as my late mother's marriage certificate although there are in the collection many wedding photos from which I was absent because my mother and father didn't go in for premarital sex or so my mother told me soon after she discovered I'd inherited no such aversion. But my grandfathers are there in the collection in Great War uniforms and I see the features mirrors still show me even in some presumably related but to me nameless faces and I am probably the nursling captured on the laps of several women who as often happened in the 1950s when hair was regularly permed look confusingly alike. You wouldn't know me then but might recognise in a few group photos snapped in one or another south London garden the longhaired youth too big for his boots or as was also said a clever clogs who'd learnt recently to look as if he didn't mean at that or any future moment to be caught in the vicinity. But this only partly accounts for my frequent absence in my late mother's photo collection.

Palaeontological, re the art of flight:

1. Mr Hawkins' pterodactyl
designed for the grounds
of the Crystal Palace
we meet again if only
in your case no pun intended
as a 1:30 scale model
on a shelf outside the
gents in the Bath Royal
Literary & Scientific Institution.

2. When you go on time travels watch out for
Heracles Inexpectata half as tall as you
& weighing in at 1 stone. Don't go near him.
That parrot could tear limb from limb.
Don't ask him questions such as was it his
taste for local meat or his weight or height
or if his wings were too weak or that
he hadn't been taught the word for flight.

3. I'd imagined that if an archaeopteryx
circled overhead she'd cast a huge shadow
but an archaeopteryx was no bigger
than a magpie with a tail just as long
although unlike a magpie or a pheasant
sharp teeth. But like a pheasant she
probably only flew under threat
& probably like pheasants too late.

▷

4. The Rodrigues Solitaire was proud-necked
with one club of a bone on each wing-tip.
The noisy male was a champ skull-cracker
although cousin to the dodo & now but
sadly unlike some other supremacists also extinct.

5. The earliest identified species of pterosaur
who took flight about 10 million years before but
lived to watch over the first dinos grow up
left bones & teeth too airy & light
to lift from their deathbed
a Triassic sand dune in Utah
a state renowned for its interest in family trees.

6. Batrachopus grandis: a crocodile
who ran like T.Rex leaving footprints
but no bones in South Korea —
Imagine him with wings
Imagine him tetchy as an ostrich
strutting his stuff in a safari park.
Imagine but don't look.
He'll either peck your eyes out
or snack on your wing mirror.

7. Another time birds grew four legs.
Some species had fingers & thumbs.
You should've seen what the chimpcrows,
neighbour, did to hellhounds like you.

On the Sea of

Verrazzano who sailed north past the Outer Banks
and thought he saw an ocean, three thousand miles
of it and then some, over to the west. Verrazzano gave
thanks and sent word back to King Francis his master
so that it showed on the sea-charts for forty or more years.
Hakluyt believed in it and probably also the beloved
Sir Walter in his dreams of Roanoke. All the trouble
with the locals came after that and then starvation but
there was always measles in the white man's favour.
But supposing one crew or another did cross that
Sea of Verrazzano would it greatly have improved
Sino-European relations? To the Chinese the only
difference would have been that these men arrived
in the opposite direction from the usual merchants
and they who'd sold luxuries to Romans and Sultans
could afford to be casual. Other empires came and went
and so sooner or later would the mariners of Verrazzano.

You can no more always remember which war
than not wonder when you're reading for example
George Barker whether you've ever in his sense
written anything resembling a poem. But I wasn't
thinking of the war he got through somehow
but leaving aside several hundred smaller and
supposedly civil affairs the one before that
which tended to conflate poetry with verse and if
the seafront memorial at Aberystwyth is anything
to go by to rhyme a jaunty triumphal wreath
with at the foot of a morbidly phallic column
a raunchy siren's excited nipples. Was she that war's
Helen? A pinup heralding another round of dynastic
pingpong? Buxom muse for boys to invoke
in Delville Wood before most were potted among
trees flaring up through the daylong downpour
& the lucky such as Harold Macmillan escaped
with a limp & altho' he was invalided out & missed it
Sassoon with durable rage against senile Blimps?
The scorn directed in 1918 at homecoming
soldiers predicted by Ford Madox Ford was as
shortly overlooked as the refusal to advance on Berlin
which would have given the troops denied immediate
demob something to occupy at least themselves.
Let's not go into anything as modish as counter-
factual histories except to say that young Auden
& Isherwood's nights out at Noster's Cottage might
have been scuppered but to return to this present
Armistice Day an ex prime minister I need not name's
promised to deliver no doubt at some length his
vindication of whichever war the latest one is.

Although reigns of sixty & more years
are a topic these days no-one seems
to remember much about George the 3rd
except that he lost the American colonies
and then his mind. It's said George the 3rd
looked kindly on that failed assassin who
was bound for Bedlam because he foresaw
that a straightjacket also awaited him
and while or perhaps because the slant
of his forehead shown by Gillray suggests
something missing it seems George the 3rd
even thought he meant well by going out
eyeballing peasants. He probably did
pinch as many pennies as Peter Pindar
could tongue-twist in rhyme but despite
the fancy of a king's two bodies one or
both in his case satirically buggered
I doubt he expected so to resurrect as
to justify the right to always pack a gun.
You must have met him more than once
in William Blake's prophecies, the liberty
of Wilkes and Paine's common sense
and where would we be without that trio
but allowing that it was an age frantic as
ours for news and comment as constantly
repeated as annoying quirks of speech
and not forgetting the quarrels of the Foxes
and the Pitts it's still a puzzle why a king
should be so often depicted surprised
at stool as Farmer George. Perhaps

▷

in those privy moments he saw himself
manuring his kingdom and so let's hope
that in his purplest visions of futurity
the cause of his indisposition wasn't
GM crops. Booksellers loved him.
His legacy's mostly in the BL and BM.

———

Now that cookery's been clichéd as soft porn
Grub Street's redeveloped as a fashion website.
Perhaps Orwell denied George Gissing was a prophet
because he'd pilfered his notion that renouncing money's
to obsess about money although he did acknowledge
that Gissing foresaw what 'literature' which as he
(Gissing) remarked was a late 19th century concept
would end up as. *New Grub Street* gets four & a half
stars on Amazon & probably as many readers per annum
despite our liking for very dark places. But perhaps it's
the original Grub Street the fashionistas envisage,
a re-enactment of the *Dunciad*, models gushing down
Fleet sewage at top 21st century speed but not fast
enough: Grub Street Fashion's already given way
to GrubStreet Inc a nonprofit creative writing center
& a blog where Chef bakes towering whimsical cakes.

———

Revisionist historians of the Great War
warn us to distrust memoirs telling tales
of wading knee-deep in mud along trenches
battalion diaries reported well-drained & swept
clean after breakfast. In revisionist histories
it didn't rain as often as those rarely
lice-ridden veterans liked to complain
& the half-dead were promptly stretchered
off the field so that Nomansland wouldn't
sound like cattle at market to Kitchener's
recruits on the second day at Loos.
Even before masks were perfected
gas wasn't so bad & no one was to blame
if it blew back. How come old lads lied?
There's no telling that. The ammo of
revisionist historians is quantified in
percentage terms e.g. numbers of Brits
killed by the enemy or died of other causes or
survived minus eyes or bollocks or limbs in
proportion to lighter armies in lesser conflicts
proving that the Great War sums don't add up
to as many as many of us think. The 67
thousand Blighters gone bonkers for life
no more count than the poets who
Gordon Corrigan asserts 'wrote for money'.
For Gurney to save in the loony bin or
Owen in the grave: 'gloom was always a winner'.

—

A postcard I bought at John Rylands
I'd supposed was an image of St George
& the Dragon. The square-jawed horse
resembles St George's as often depicted
and there's something in the way
the rider thrusts his spear as politely as
an English Christian gentleman should.
I hadn't noticed that his victim is
elfin & probably female of the species
an amiable creature not a macabre dancer
or grinnygog hellcat grilling local wife-
swappers moneybags & thieves on the
wall of Chaldon village church. The verso
of the postcard says she is the angel
of death from a Syrian MS and perhaps
death showed a friendlier face in Syria
in those days. But some hero had to
kill her anyway in spite of her willing
& winning smile we're still told we must
not in any circumstance acknowledge.

(interlude: Afternoon Tea)

The only sound in the conservatory came from the shuffling steps of a newcomer pushing a three-wheeled walking frame heavily before her. A younger but not young man and woman possibly her son and his wife closely followed.

The newcomer sank with loud breath from walking frame to armchair. The possible son and his wife sat down to left and right.

Three women occupied armchairs set side by side against the opposite windows.

'Hello Muriel' called the newcomer, her tone inviting no response.

Brief silence before the newcomer told the possible son and his wife so that Muriel might hear 'She never answers.'

Now the light quick footfall of a young woman.

'Tea or coffee, Edith?' Slumped Edith was asleep. 'Muriel?' 'Tea' replied Muriel, straight-backed, without moving eyes or head. 'Margery?' 'Coffee.' A flimsy but glossy magazine hid Margery's face.

Coffee for the newcomer, tea for the possible son and wife.

Edith without waking muttered annoyance at the chink of cup in saucer. The young woman went on to serve the other teas and coffees.

Did Muriel blink while sipping her tea? She did not. Had her back slightly relaxed? It had not. Was it only her severity of haircut which seemed mannish? It was not but it was not for this reason that Margery drinking coffee raised her magazine one or two inches.

The newcomer demanded a pill which she lengthily explained she'd forgotten to take with her dinner three hours ago.

The young woman smiled and said 'I'll bring it with the cakes.' Off she went, soon returning plate in hand.

'Here's your cake, Edith.' 'Go away' mumbled Edith. Her face may have been troubled by momentary unwanted waking or else it was her dream perhaps time unwillingly regained.

The others received cakes and the newcomer her pill in silence disturbed by Thank Yous to her left and right. Muriel might have moved her head when Margery flipped her magazine to the next flimsy page but did not.

The possible son and wife smiled back at the young woman leaving with partly emptied plate.

notes towards a poem for Paul Merchant:

Those years I spent driving around England
because every small town had two or three
secondhand bookshops with the chance
of a snip I was always in two minds
one a memorised roadmap and the other
enhancing the map with an added dimension
I wouldn't pretend I could describe but
presenting a land part seen part imagined
inhabited by unidentified beasts and not entirely
human men & women I tried later to picture so
flagrantly out of perspective as to disturb some
sensitive souls. Now I think again of Mercator
recovering the Earth from the charms of
the mappaemundi but seeing it still
from the Lowlands. That centre even now of
but a little to the west as we see it from here
our familiar projection. It could have been
another way but at the time not much —
Mercator's penpal Dee had already envisaged
the British Empire and reclamation at last
of the once & future king's farflung domains
now reduced to the relics I'd either seen
or imagined when driving around England.

Dear Paul I'm writing a book
called Remarks of Uncertain Consequence
so perhaps in such a context
this is the poem and not notes towards.
Once I'd have squeezed it till it squealed
but the consequence of that too was uncertain.

PS Facts and yarns do get skewed
when we're writing poems.
It seems there was a priest
in the court of Norway
who told Jacob Cnoyen that
K.Arthur found the NW passage.
When Mercator read this
he passed it on to Dee
although Dee surely knew
that Secretary Cromwell
had used Geoffrey of Monmouth's
tale of Arthur's imperium to back
his master Henry's case against Rome.
But however it went
one thing led to another.

Archival note. The author presumably refers to the 1533 Act in Restraint of Appeals: 'Where by divers sundry old authentic histories and chronicles it is manifestly declared and expressed that this realm of England is an Empire, and so hath been accepted in the world', as quoted in 2012 by Sir John Redwood MP in support of the campaign to leave the EU. The 'old authentic histories' almost wholly derive from Geoffrey of whom as early as 1190 William of Newburgh observed 'it is quite clear that everything this man wrote about Arthur and his successors, or indeed his predecessors from Vortigern onwards, was made up, partly by himself and partly by others'; and 'only a person ignorant of ancient history would have any doubt about how shamelessly and impudently he lies in almost everything.'

(notes on absence continued)

In the photos of my father's father in my late mother's
collection his hair is combed into a middle and exactly
straight parting as many footballers combed theirs in the
interwar years. But my father's father so far as I know
for my father never spoke to me of his father who as I
remember lay ill in bed the few times we met was not a
footballing man. My mother once told me that during his
long unemployment in the 1930s he served as secretary to
the Clapham Communist Party but when I reminded her
of this some years later she seemed greatly surprised if
not offended and firmly denied it. How or why she didn't
notice that my father's ashes deposited in the Surrey &
Sussex Crematorium are designated in not my father's
but my father's father's name I cannot explain. A cursory
scan of my late mother's photo collection shows that my
father slicked back his hair in the manner of footballers
famous in the postwar years but so far as I know my father
although he liked to watch football was himself no player.

add. notes on heritage

1. Richard Crookback's skull
no sexier than anyone's
despite its unusual
hole to the rear
                    but its owner
called in Leicester & York
'one of the most significant
in our national history'
because his tax reforms
'survive to the modern day'
no doubt as one Congressman
said of Mr Trump's concessions
concealing some Deficit Spin.

2. Browsing the latest Tudor
Featured Products you may
wonder how far the Anne Boleyn
Bottle Cap Style Necklace goes to
explain the English Reformation
or whether the AB Perfect Weight
Scoop T-Shirt was sufficient cause
for the Dissolution of the Monasteries
but Henry the 8th was a likely sucker
for 3 for the price of 2 and so the AB
Lightweight Flowy Racerback Tank
might be held responsible for
the demolition of more art than
Islamic State has yet accomplished.

▷

3a. Easter Sunday service at St Albans
opens with praise for that martyr
without mention that because
he needed for his meditation
Godly silence in the woods
he banished (or worse — the tales
don't tell) the unmerciful nightingales.

3b. St Alban would welcome the earlier springs
of the 21st century in which nightingales' wings
have shortened to allow for a brood of 3 nestlings
an adaptation which also shortens their chance
of surviving migration. With resultant silence
in the remnant woods of southern England
we can expect augmentation of saintly meditation.

4. Those dopes used dope! —
Neanderthal News Flash —
got their aspirin from poplars
& penicillin somehow —
there's no ignoring that
while homo sapiens goes down
in its own estimation
Neanderthals go up.

5. New Grange DNA shows that in Ireland
& as tales passed down thro' the Christian Era
until they reached James Joyce also record
neolithic lords & ladies researchers call
'the ruling elite' without taboo or ado coupled
bro & sis. Mind your language, researchers.
To the Irish 'the ruling elite' means English.
No matter when. In England it's another story.

6. Woodlice? They aren't such a horror
if you call them gramfer-gravies.
As species go they're staunch survivors
with more names than anyone remembers.
So, Apothecary, please, don't crush them
with pestle & mortar — don't flush them
in warm oil down my ears whatever
Gerard or Culpeper or somebody said.
My tinnitus isn't so bad. I can wait.
I'll get peace & quiet when I'm dead.

7. The converted asylums
on the outer rim of London
weren't a theme I was pursuing
in the wake of Iain Sinclair
but they pursue me. Reading
Hilary Mantel's *Giving Up the Ghost*
I imagined her living at Colney Hatch
until she said her conversion's on
the southern axis east of Cane Hill.
If you know that book you'll
remember her good friends
the gargoyles on her balcony.
Presumably the younger breed
protective of the churches
of the Gothic Revival but
some must have preferred
a more convivial roost.

▷

8. Footnotes to poems tend to ramble in
much the same way the ghosts of the
Napoleonic Wars kept shuffling about
in the 20th century. In 1950s playgrounds
Boney was still as big a bogey as Hitler despite
the testicular song to the tune of the Colonel
which in '51 was the first ever sung by
a computer. Boney whose familiar ghost
was like Julius Caesar's Alexander the Great.
Time's a river which flows backwards in
footnotes & underworld, tell that to Heraclitus
or the Marines as English sailors mainly
men pressganged to fight Boney liked to say.

A cortical homunculus
is a distorted representation
of the human body
based on a neurological map
of the areas and proportions
of the human brain
processing motor functions
for different parts of the body

first identified in the 20th century
by Wilder Graves Penfield
& referred to by Freud
in *The Ego and the Id* as
'the "cortical homunculus"
of the anatomists
which stands on its head
sticks up its heels
faces backwards and has its
speech–area on the left-hand side'

The Ego and the Id
being the development of
Beyond the Pleasure Principle
in which Freud introduced
into psychoanalysis
the drive towards death
without reference to
(and perhaps this was also
overlooked by despite his
name Wilder Graves Penfield)
the uses and abuses of

▷

Homunculus Mandrake
by an earlier anatomist
the author of *Death's Jest-Book*
whose surname derives from
the Welsh for the grave

The fun about SF novels written mid 20th century
is they got so much wrong. Predicting digital tech but
describing machines we'd send to municipal dump
or Antiques Roadshow at the same time supposing
we'd by now be crossing thousands of light years in
a few Earth minutes and colonising faraway planets
virgin as America once seemed when we've only
established a few building sites on Mars. But they
got a few things right. Multinational franchise,
worldwide surveillance at the mercy of mutant
viral double agents, psycho politicians in denial
of overpopulation & global fry-up. Perfection
of labour & death camps in the name of good health
but how Czarist and old-style Colonial was that
dreamtime spaced out to hide the heart of darkness.
Mr Kurtz he racist or other one fearing any other
because any may be some other's keeper? Every
blank on a map figured as a planet known only
to itself but its virginity lost long before alien
space- or slaveships arrived. You can call it either
imagination's failure or self-evident truth that
an Earthling colony will mirror the Homeland's
parochial ignorance and paranoiac hatreds but
in case you haven't got it read some more SF
written in those optimisty days before
Dystopia was granted planning permission.

Message Parlour Miscreants:

As if the seeing mind by my saying's mine to find.

Momentous monotony: reality as proven satire.

A testament's estimate, knowledge on a knife-edge.

Persecuted by precursors but eased by erasure.

As biota and mutagens show: there are gaps.

A parabola of parables or else a palaver.

In advance of the broken promise: here lies N or M.

A remote meteor, probably, or intercept chatter.

Telephonemesis: even a clone can believe he's the one.

There's no climbing out of the pitfalls of ekphrasis.

Hormones considered as omen replacement.

A recipe for intense jelly, a precipice of awkward treacle.

A despot's deposit in the geologic record: a reptile replies.

Was that a flashback or a premonition?

Duty's in the I of the beholden.

Devices of forgotten purpose, caustic acoustics, banal epiphanies.

There are no long paragraphs in nature.

One moment a stronghold, a stranglehold the next.

The soul unseated? Nauseated? By holistic hostility?

When there's a greed to disagree: digress.

I heard it from the journalists who drink in The Toxin & Icon.

re disambiguation: Calypso

to cover / to conceal / to deceive
'singing' although not in the Afro-
Caribbean style 'as she strolls about
with a golden shuttle' she enchants
etymology as much as Odysseus.
That Latinus was either her or Circe's
son only shows that she and Circe
have always been lightly confused
but it's certainly Calypso who
laments that gods revile goddesses
for letching after toyboy mortals
and she has a point. We needn't
for now go into all the goings-
on of Zeus. We're told to compare
Calypso with Siduri 'who plies the
inconsolable wanderer' known
in her time as Gilgamesh with
drink and drugs until he's so off
his chump that he chops down
trees to make a raft and set sail
for a place beyond the sea co-
ordinates uncertain but possibly
in the West Indies 'reserved for
a special class of honoured people'

Dear Mister Graham

What's the language using us for now?
The Urban Dictionary defines 'jible'
as 'a jean bible made of denim'
since 'denim is the holiest of fabrics'.
The author may not have read
in your 'Many Without Elegy'
To sail against spout of this monumental loss
That jibles with no great nobility its cause
and can't have known any more than I
despite a smart crevasse-proof phone
which lets (if I had one & I bet
nor would you) the language use us
any time or place it chooses
that Scots dialect 'jible'
means 'drunkenly babble'.

———

Too sadly named
Farewell Crapper
of Malin Bridge
buried aged 4

in the churchyard
of Nicholas patron
saint of children
in High Bradfield

sharing his grave
with his laterborn
brother & parents
who survived him

till the night the
Dale Dyke Dam
11 March 1864
on its first filling

as what one report
called 'a useful
warning' burst
sending 3M cubic

metres of water
down Loxley Valley
flooding over Joseph
Crapper the cobbler

▷

& his wife & son
Joseph's cottage
leaving no trace
but story still told

and you'll remember
the dam's site when
driving from Bradfield
past Dungworth

another note on heritage & re disambiguation:

Crapper from *OE* 'croppe' 'a mower or field labourer'
'common in Lancs where the Crappers held a family seat'
'This unusual and interesting name' for a fruit- or
veg-picker or reaper of corn 'croppe' elsewhere said to
mean 'swelling' or 'head of a plant' and so 'croppen'
to pick or pluck. 'Surnames became necessary when
governments introduced Poll Tax', remember that?
The notion that 'crap' meaning shit alludes to the
sanitary engineer Tom Crapper of South Yorks is
sometimes blamed on the childish humour of GIs
stationed in England during WWII who saw his name
on many a cistern but maybe they knew Dutch 'krappen'
or *OF* 'crappe' 'rejected matter, chaff' leading us back to
the fields of old England before according to the *OED*
a privy became known as a 'crapping kcn'
around 1846 when Tom was a lad aged ten.

———

Leonard Smithers doesn't usually appear
in the rollcall of Worthies of Sheffield
even though he was Sheffield born & bred
and set up as a local solicitor in 1884

perhaps because he is somewhat better
known as the publisher of Burton's erotica
not to mention *The Ballad of Reading Gaol*
or the poems of Dowson & Arthur Symons

names rarely dropped in the precincts
of Cutlers' Hall. Smithers is more often
consigned to Soho where the Society
for the Suppression of Vice hunted him

down and ensured that by 1900 despite
good sales he was bankrupt. Seven years
later he overdosed on J. Collis Browne's
cough mixture which as I remember

druggies still queued up for at a Kings
Cross pharmacy in 1969. This happened
in Parsons Green a suburb of west London
I mean Leonard Smithers' suicide. If

he'd chosen Parsons Cross a suburb of
north Sheffield then he might be at last
enrolled in the short title lists of Sheffield
publishers radical for sundry other causes.

The lightweight
two-wheeled
horse-drawn
war chariot

'the world's first
complex machine
and the first
advanced weapon'

invincible until
the other side
came up with
the javelin.

Fast forward
to 1915 and
Little Willie
the first tank

a machine as
it turned out
less lethal than
the family car.

———

Another loop in the
late nights of an editor
& perplexed bibliographer
'Perhaps it is in volume 3'

Bill Griffiths wrote in his
apparently nearly last poem
'Monkey' file dated 26.7.07
& looking back I wonder

even though I'm thinking
of a different & woefully
posthumous Griffiths vol 3
whether that's perhaps so

of umpteen poems
threaded out by that
labyrinthine mind I've
tried years to follow

    ['Will I be in time
    to stop it?' Bill asks
    & then remarking 'No
    good can come of this'

    but there again 'What new
    adventures await our heroes?'
    before 'My poem ends': 'Future
    episodes suddenly stopped.']

(notes on absence para. 3)

I'd expected the absence in my late mother's photo collection of my cousins on my father's side unless there were a few murky snaps of a shared day out in Worthing during a rare cessation of family hostilities. But a wet day in Worthing's a bad day for snaps and we had nothing better to do than lob pebbles at the waves on the incoming tide. One of mine hit cousin Grahame's head hard enough for everyone and in particular his sister Christine to claim his life was in danger and for me to be accused of unforgivable malice even though I'd always been cackhanded at throwing pebbles but this possibly led to the subsequent resumption of hostilities between our family and the family of my father's sister Doris. It must have agonised cousin Christine not to cross my path for nearly fifty years because as I quickly discovered when we did meet again in a Haywards Heath hotel after visiting my mother in the nearby Princess Royal Hospital she'd been anxious to tell me 'Your Mum killed our Nan'. I could have replied 'Your Mum tried to kill my Dad' but refrained. The murder weapon her Mum selected was a carving or it may have been no more than a bread knife and this happened so my late mother told me in the dismal third-floor flat in Grafton Square in Clapham where my Dad and sister Doris lived with their father and mother and was the reason my Mum as she admitted during one of our rows when I'd begun to think I had a mind of my own felt so sorry for my Dad that she married him sooner than planned or expected in that era of prolonged engagements. Perhaps she told me this hoping I'd not wondered but why should I. In any case a decade or so later our Nan had wearied of this world

▷

because the noisy Russian satellites wouldn't let her sleep and perhaps that afternoon my Mum had to hurry home to cook my Dad's dinner leaving our Nan in bed in her flat in Tulse Hill without realising our Nan who was certainly a hypochondriac needed hospital treatment. But there may have been more to this tale with or without embellishments by cousin Christine's Mum who was married to a man who mistook himself for Liberace.

———

'The Anyplace app gives open access
to anything of yours you suppose secure
as proof that computer hacking's
the twentyfirst century equivalent
of psychoanalysis'
     'O shut up'
anyone's friend Dr Thanatos splutters
'That's the super-ego trying to conceal
guile & disguise by guile & disguise
as poets do —
    & a remark of
more uncertain consequence
than I'd expect from even you'

———

So the harvest was at last gathered in,
winejars sealed, pomegranates stored
& tho' they'd lit the woodburner they'd
put on winter woollies & the table talk
diverted to their host's prize mural
some guests fancying Leda & some
others the swan while the slavegirls
between courses passed from hand
to hand cherished pick-me-up crystals
scarab amulets & amber so that nobody
noticed the bricky outdoors with a stick
of charcoal scrawling his name on his
handiwork & adding the date this day of
October not August as a monk misread
Pliny's letter when the lava from Vesuvius
came a-rolling & a-tumbling & with
the temperature rising beyond 500C
one victim's brain turned into glass
a phenomenon usually ascribed to the
irrational dread some melancholics suffer
tho' in their case while they're still
alive & affecting the whole body

———

The Thames Barrier didn't show up
in George the 3rd's visions and so
he drifted into Ballard's dystopia
& witnessed the Great Flood of London
which the Thames Barrier now winter
rain's falling in Greenland and fiftysix
lakes have formed beneath the icecap
will probably not avert. As the books
fluttered around in the submerged libraries
George the 3rd dived down to snatch
as many as he could but almost certainly
flung politicians' memoirs back in the drink.
'It was always my duty to protect science'
he explained when he resurfaced
and 'I never made a friend of a Minister.'

'Thomas the Tank' —
I heard it when I'd only
popped in the kitchen
for a fill-up of coffee —
'was a gravy train'

and perhaps unrelatedly
but after all this happened
in an offshore island
of Europe in 2018

daffodils & deadfalls
neighbourly as mushrooms
far-bidden pageants or
murmur of Myrmidons
lied to but relied on

as we've said ever since we
viewed us from the moon
a blue planet not to be
mistaken for Schlaraffia

itself not to be mistaken
for the boys' club founded
in Prague in 1859 but the
earthly 16th century paradise
also called Cockaigne

where if you walk out
on the luckiest of mornings
along a pastry pavement
past barley sugar houses

either a fried pigeon or
a grilled goose might
despite the sanctions
of Universal Credit
fly straight into
your starving mouth

———

Odi et amo
in another context —
howler-hunters
compulsive nitpickers
hawkeyed errorists —
what
would I be
without you

(the otherness of
once published poems
with their abandoned
animus and muses
their amenities
not so much non-
entities as ammonites
authored by absence)

((either copy to clipboard
or for 'nothingness'
read 'nostalgia'
evergreen or overgrown
but less gloomy than
some of these remarks
once written must seem))

(((don't think I don't
remind myself sometimes
I might look to you like

text scissored & pasted
on a good bad news day
dropped into then
pulled from a hat)))

———

'life, after all' mused Henry Green
'is one discrepancy after another' —
I might have snaffled that as
companion to the Gellner epigraph
but one's enough. In the talks
he broadcast soon after he stopped
writing novels Green also observed
that words by themselves
'can mean almost anything'
and stressed that for the novelist
and for that matter in life as we live it
context is all. Green apparently
when he wasn't revisiting *Arabia Deserta*
but not *The Dawn in Britain* read
at least in his later years a novel
or two every day but poetry
never. Perhaps because novels need
context to make words either say what
they mean or mean what they say while
poems jump it for ends of their own.

The youngly fair dungareed moptop
testing rusty saw on a small block of wood
in the garden of his granddad's
semidetached in Georgia Road
in an area of Thornton Heath
all whose streets were named after
for no apparent reason
states of the USA —

that house which another photo showed
the undetonated bomb which
dropped through its garage roof
& the gang of so he was told
POWs either Jerries or Eye-Ties
gathered round it as a trophy
they'd defused & could safely
with shy grins show the camera —

this was during the war which had happened
not long ago & the young chippy supposed
for no apparent reason
had happened at exactly a time
& time after time before he was reborn

or so he thought later & often
in the garden of his dad's terrace house
half a mile from Georgia Road
in an area of Thornton Heath
all whose streets were named after
for unfortunate reasons
heroes of the Empire

▷

where Dougie shinned up the tree
next door above the Anderson shelter
with binoculars trained on the first Sputnik
a word which while Anderson shelters
were removed to museums awaited revival
as the Russian riposte to Western vaccines
against viruses depicted as spiky spacecraft

——

'Some civic routine one never learns.'
Gurney's talking here about veterans
returned from the front with nowhere to go
'walking town to town sore in borrowed tatterns'
in the 1920s. Forty years later we'd meet
the survivors bedded down in Spa Hill Woods
or at midnight with elbows on the sausage stall counter
their backs turned to the traffic & shrunk pond
where the gibbet used to be. Funny old geezers
shapeless as their coats & frayed as their trousers
with nobody knew what in their knapsacks.
They mostly chuntered to themselves in their own lingo.
We never asked them who they were or where
they'd come from. Gurney's poem's called 'Strange Hells'.

——

After a morning's footie in Grange Park
when papers were full of the Profumo Affair
me & my mates yack-yack-yacked about
what the 'whipping' Stephen Ward was said
to enjoy actually meant. We all had ideas but
none of us supposed corporal punishment
was anyone's fancy. We'd had enough
of that from the trembling hands not to
mention stretched flies & shaking knees of
canehappy headmasters & chemistry teachers.
In any case the doings of Miss Keeler &
Miss Rice-Davies the Mandy of our dreams
tickled us more than either Dr Ward's pleasures
or Supermac's imminent fall with its promise
of the end of government by chums described
inexplicably to Thornton Heath no-hopers as
Old Etonians. That was the joyous prospect
papers whipped up. They were only kidding.

Demob men still scouting for boys
after the Boer War & even after
WWII marching their troops on
church parade led by bugles &
drums or singing by camp fires
their Parlay Voos & of rats big as
cats in the Quartermaster's Stores
& 'Remember, Mac, the spade trick?'
'Course, Skip, how could I forget?'
so we'd hear again how when one
of your pals went out for a crap
you'd catch his shit in a spade
& pull it away so your pal had to
wonder if his bowels deceived him
oh the fun they'd had & now after
Lights Out prowling from tent to tent
all ears for a lad begging his mate
'Finish it for me, Les, finish it for me.'

(further notes on absence)

The earliest photo of her father in my late mother's collection is a full-length studio portrait in which he looks
about twelve years old although it's hard to judge because
he'd been dressed up in mostly grown-up clothes as if for
the first time and his black jacket worn over a matching
waistcoat with prominent watch chain is slightly too big
while his three-quarter-length grey trousers seem to acknowledge he's still half a boy. The next is another studio
portrait in which he wears his Royal Flying Corps uniform and cap while he carries a baton in the crook of his
left elbow. He seems awkwardly balanced on the arm of a
chair in which his fiancée Beatrice sits engulfed in a formi-
dable gown black in the photo. This double portrait may
have formally announced their engagement although their
grave expressions might have alarmed their families and
friends. Then there's the wedding portrait with Beatrice
in white and with veil raised above her headdress to de-
note her changed status and Syd which was my mother's
father's name still in uniform but capless. They were both
under five feet tall and Beatrice again sits while Syd stands
but this has the disturbing effect of making Syd seem elfin and his bride a giantess. There are as you'd expect in
my late mother's collection many photos of Beatrice and
Syd from their years in Battersea and when they'd moved
south to Mitcham then Thornton Heath and at last escaping from south London to Shirley on the border between
Surrey and Kent but they were mostly taken on special
occasions requiring Sunday best clothes and behaviour
which means that the couple I particularly loved as my
mother's mother and father are also in a distinct and lam-
entable way absent. And yet I always recognise Syd by his

strangely self-effacing smile and thick silver hair with the widow's peak which my mother inherited and also Eric her brother so that in later years I couldn't look at Eric without seeing Syd. But the photos don't show the homelier man in his oilsplashed raincoat with the sleeves cut off to make a jerkin when he was out in his garage doing whatever he seemed constantly needing to do to keep his jalopy fit for the road while the cigarette apparently attached to his lower lip gradually burnt down to a tube of ash as I followed him around for whiffs of shared smoke. But the Beatrice in my mother's photo collection I can't recognise at all. She seems mannish if not asexual and although she tries to smile the effort defeats her. She bears no resemblance to the woman who often called me Eric as if I stood in place of her beloved but faraway son and perhaps for that reason was more motherly to me than my late mother. That woman is entirely absent from my mother's photo collection.

A riddle:

In advance of your seventieth birthday
the Driver & Vehicle Licensing Agency
will ask you for a mugshot. Geraldine
says mine from the photobooth looks
like Eric Burdon as he used to look
reminding us of the Frenchman who
asked me was I really Eric B that night
in the lift at the Columbia Hotel after
some josher's underpants caught fire
& Grumps night clerk Douglas turned
us out on the street & watched us mill
around & shiver half an hour before
he let us back in. Earlier that evening
I suppose because I'd slanted the brim
of my old grey trilby low on my face
because I always feel edgy in London
an anxious passerby who couldn't have
read the obituaries wanted to know
if I was Joseph Beuys. However will
my mugshot help the DVLA identify
me as the licensed man at the wheel?
Am I asking a lot to ask Who am I?

on heritage again:

1. The ladies of the Restoration court
whose sport was to ride dressed as lords
gave Pepys the hots at first & then not.
He doesn't say if these huntresses
claimed by crossdressing men's rights
nor if rakehells prettified & posing
as patched belles claimed women's.
The rule in the Restoration court
was no matter what you think or see
shut your mouth. As we're told must we.

2. It's true Sir Peter Lely wasn't Titian
but was his Nell Gwyn so 'ungainly'?
She was certainly worth Old Rowley's toss
probably five times a day if Nell & Moll
& Poll & La Belle were on the pull elsewhere.
The cupid portraying her li'l baby Charles
lifting the veil over Nell's none too fore-
fended place shows wit but was it Lely's?
Was it his to depict the former Mrs Palmer
as the Virgin Mary? The bewitching Babs
was Lady Castlemaine by then & uncrowned
queen aka quim of the copulated kingdom
but if of Heaven too then whose exactly?
The quip's not so much cock- as cackhanded.
Lely was neither Titian nor a politician.
His station was to celebrate the Restoration.

▷

3. When Lady Castlemaine to tease
her Lord the King for a jolly
evening's court theatre played
bridegroom bedding the model
for Britannia Frances Stewart
Charles as expected stepped up
to the plate although the dish
on the plate was for Charles
a cold fish. How perplexing for
a king to be denied his wish
but the tease for historians
is whether the wicked Lady C
did rightfully or wrongfully
claim young Britannia's cherry.

———

Why did Yeats Eliot & Pound
pretend in their youth
to be old guys?
How useful a disguise?
How profound a truth?
If you're young Discuss.

— That funny old codger
fussing in his garden
about which plant goes where
& what counts as a weed
was a poet once
and some days even now
you'll see him pull
not 'those girls' but
a notebook from his pocket.
Still scribbling'n'quibbling.
Still saying he intends
to get it right in the end
face up and phrase perfect.

add. notes

[p.15]
'Send him to Colney Hatch'
may have been a loose translation
of 'Send him to Anticyra'
for a dose of helleborus niger
causing gut-rot and depression
if he can't get that
through the usual channels.

[p.24, 'Palaeontological' 7]
Our neighbour complains we keep her
under supervision. Untrue
but if only, neighbour, our vision were
super enough to obliterate you.

[p.25]
Probably there was such a sea as
Verrazzano claimed but 66 million
years before he thought he saw it.
It was that sea which carried the
tsunami from Chicxulub north
to Dakota floating corpses of
fish & dinos blitzed by molten
vapourised rock. This wasn't
for them the slow wintry death
it was eventually for some.
Next bulletin shortly to report
the surge in ocean heat content
& consequent increase in global
sea level risen 3.7mm in the past
12 months. Probably a future sea
Verrazzano had not envisaged.

[p.41, 'A cortical homunculus']
Let us also consider the Beast of Beddau
a quarter-inch millipede thriving in the spoil
of the derelict Cwm Coke Works. Its eyes
have eight lenses & its body's ghostly white
as if only captured by enlarging an old-
fashioned negative. That's not to say that
the Beast of Beddau hasn't future prospects
even though its stomping ground's name's
another derivation from the Welsh for 'grave'.

[p.51, 'The lightweight ...]
Little Willie was only less lethal
to some & in the long run. Best
not be stuck in sucking mud
when Willie headed your way.
As for the name of the species:
when lads used to quenching thirst in
greenscummed pisspools heard that
the newfangled camouflaged objects
were 'tanks' they in hope of a supply
of pissfree water rejoiced. How could
any lad guess the word was intended
to deceive not him but the enemy,
a nickname for machines also
called Land Creepers or Crabs,
'a cross between a turtle &
a submarine' in which parched
& unfortunate lads might fry.

▷

[p.57, 'The Thames Barrier ...']
George the 3rd's extensive library
may have included those pamphlets
published June 1523 predicting the
flood of London next Feb the 1st
which sent citizens heading north
& south to set up their tents as far
away from the Thames as Croydon
& Waltham Abbey. Nothing much
happened as it happened that Feb
the 1st but those prophecies might
have nonetheless stuck & festered in
the mind of a bibliophile & maybe
addict reader such as George the 3rd.

first last words from the message parlour:

Unless everyone misheard
Abū Nuwās' big mouth reckoned
the Prophet would prefer
a Baghdad bar to a holiday in Mecca.
+
'RAF bunker to open early for autism shopping.'
(A *former* RAF bunker; and *despite protests*.)
((Semicolons described as semiconductors.))
+
Poolside in the garden of a luxury hotel
on an island beyond the Pillars of Hercules
a jacuzzi called Hokusai in several languages.
+
If there was a hope she nurtured
it seems the compliment was not returned.
+
Forgive me. I just meant to ask
if there's a difference in farts
between cows in their millions
& a planetful of vegans
dieting on onions & beans.
+
Were you as weirdly confused
as you wearily & wordily confessed?
Expecting news of a coup d'état
or just dropping in for a cup of tea?

▷

+
Four or five years before the catastrophe
two women less transparent of body than mind
stood in Tate Britain chattering and blocking
the view of three small Schwitters collages
one in her pinch-perfect Home Counties drawl
telling the other 'Now *every*one's joining UKIP.'
+
Knitting & unknitting these
nitpicked words night after night.
'You're just shooting the breeze.'
I do & don't deny it.

I was in a radio studio in Hell
& the technicians were playing back
their recent recording of *The Text
of Shelley's Death* with actors best
known from The Archers distributing
the voices. Squeaky Shelley, glum
Mary, blabbermouth Trelawny,
Lord Napoleon Byron mocking
Hunt & his Hottentots, flirty Jane,
laconic half-husband Williams
& the rest. I kept saying 'Please
please. I deliberately didn't put
names to the voices. The point
is the text does the talking.'
Anxiously but luckily woke up
then dropped back to sleep
& the dream repeated itself.
Not vaguely. Word for word.
I began to doubt I'd slept a wink
then tried denying any presage.
Honest: even the boat had a
speaking part. I have so few
memorable fancies these days
I'd considered it reward for old age.

England in 2019
[*re* Ps. 5:6]

There are landlords who
although you've paid them
over the odds based

on a valuation they're not
legally obliged to disclose
to extend the lease on what

you considered your property
will charge a contingency
or exit fee of ten thousand

pounds when you sell what
you considered your property.
They're based offshore, these

landlords, although some of
their shareholders no doubt
sit in the House of Commons

representing people they'll tell
with forked tongues in cheeks
of straight faces how mortal

wealth's based on the savings
of a lifetime, the personal
possession of bricks & mortar

the sale of which after those
landlordly deductions will buy
you two years in a care home

assuming you outlive
the biblical span as they trust
you're persuaded you must.

—

'Everything is always what
another thing would be':
whatever I meant by that
in 1996 was probably right
at the time and, new year
2019, quite likely still is.

And there again
'Marginalia dead emerging'
as still happens
usually an hour or two
after midnight now & then.
As for example

A microsecond's rose
in a month of sundials
mental litter found as
venomous as them'n'us
when tomorrow's trials
are yesterday's contrails
fickle as they come and
go in likeness or likelihood

the author of which has
lately occupied himself
retyping poems he or
one of the same name
wrote forty years ago

there's no doubt about it
as Wordsworth nearly said
what starts as a boogie
ends in goodbye

for Gavin Selerie at 70
& i.m. Robert Creeley:

The ill or infirm or dead
condense the darkness
which does surround us

but if we count by decades
we still have fingers to spare
which with luck we'll not

eventually use up. I hadn't
realised that 50 years ago
on your 20th birthday

the Armstrong trio set
off for the moon when at
your prompt I spliced that

shot of the backpacked
spaceman above the festival
stage on the Isle of Wight.

Spaceman ghostlily fuzzed
to an albino ape hunched
against the moon-slag.

Stage blackened to show
only the band's white jackets.
Soon and like the spaceman

to as you say 'catch the
ferry back.' To Earth or
mainland. To 'look out

where yr going.' This long
later some questions like
darkness are not used up.

Dear Roy

It's a wonder but not always
of obligation what difference comes to.
For instance that photo on the cover
of your ghost of a paper bag.
I never saw a party table set out
on the street where I grew up
nor so many neighbours at once.
Was that the difference between Handsworth
& Thornton Heath or 1935 & '53?
Or between a Silver Jubilee & a Coronation?
You were four at the one & I was three at
the other & although you're right that some
difference is neutral there's more to come:
one of the faces in that photo's yours but even
if we'd had a street party for the Coronation
I know I'd be missing from the snaps.
I was only let peep at the cakes & paper crowns
in next door's front room. Perhaps because
seeing so many neighbours at once I cried
hard enough to be ushered or rushed home
to bed & to forget. Is that another local
suburban difference or the pre- against postwar
or north v. south? Although Handsworth's
not so far north & Thornton Heath
just south of London & we did leave to
live elsewhere. Heading north but harking back.
The rivers in both our towns were built over.
How could I tell what the party next door
meant to mean & you must have wondered

at the obligation of a Silver Jubilee.
That's what bewilders even when
we're not children. The difference
not neutral helping poems out.

more last words from the message parlour:

Suppose the quiz show contestant was right
that Mohammed went out into the desert
& met Michelangelo: but what then, what then?
+
A land without rivers such as Malta
may account for an alphabet
with several additional letters
mostly silent.
+
Old Grouch in the department store
who told me to go back to Afghanistan
probably voted to leave the EU.
+
'There're lots of egos hereabouts as Eros
remarked and no limit to the limelight.'
'Show up or be shown up's the choice.'
'Which of those is a reason to rejoice?'
'You asked me that in a different voice.'
+
Coprophage chums of Citizen Sade
haven't you heard about
the shitbergs in England's sewers?
Need I say England needs you?
+
Newfound opponents met on a golf course
one sunny afternoon without remorse
redistributing spare capital at source.
+
Apocalypsephology
as subject for future study
if there's time in the heat
of that time for retrospection.

+
Another click on the remote
shows the distant horizon
then a weary pun on 'orison'.
Did that 's' used to be
a soft 'g'? The second 'o'
an 'i' in exile? 'Origin'
which according to Foucault
Nietzsche banished as if it
were if you'll forgive my fancy
a specimen spaceman
abandoned in language long ago.

(penultimate notes on absence)

There are many photos in my mother's collection of her brother Eric and his first wife Marjorie the mother of my cousins John and Pip and in later years his second wife Cath but by then my mother only figures in a few group snaps. My mother more than once called her brother Eric's family in faraway Malvern snaphappy which the evidence bears out considering also the absence in her collection of any prints of her brother's sharply focused black and white landscape studies such as the photo of a snowbound wooden bridge in Malvern's Winter Gardens probably taken during the notorious winter of 1947/8 which held pride of place on his mother and father's living room wall until his and my mother's mother died and their father mourning the wife he'd nursed for so long entered a care home in Croydon. But there is in the collection a set of photos of my young mother in the elaborate costumes she wore when on stage with her brother Eric during his career as a magician. My mother seemed sometimes on the point of saying she felt that as her brother's assistant she was always less loved by their mother and father. The Second World War ended their theatrical career and the next photos of Eric show him in the chunky furlined jacket and boots of the RAF perhaps ready to take off on the surveillance flight to Barcelona he once told me lasted sixteen hours. He didn't tell me the purpose of this mission to neutral Barcelona but he was mainly occupied with radar research and on summer holidays when I went walking as appears in several snaps with my mother and father on the Malvern Hills we'd look down on the Radar Research Establishment where he worked according to my mother in official secret which was why he kept himself partly although playfully absent. My mother mounted the photos of their youthful career in a special album which ends with a portrait of her ventriloquist brother's dummy Horace which my mother occasionally asked after all these years to see again when we visited Eric and his family in Malvern but Eric always replied that Horace was somewhere up in the loft and couldn't for the moment be brought down and so I never had the chance to hear Horace's side of the story.

The Dulle Griet stalked
WSG & Geoffrey Hill
in as different ways as
considering their disparate
muses or notions thereof
I'd expect. Nevertheless
Mad Meg the Dulle Griet
whether by whisky or Prozac
or Netherlandish halflight
leads her conscripts to Hell.
The question is how many
hells there are & how many
notions thereof. More than
anyone can count or fancy?
Don't forget that we only
know about Graham & Hill's
encounters with Meg from
their posthumous poems.
One's choice, one by chance.
One in the London Blitz
in his undisclosed absence,
one in fearful presence at
Calgary International arrivals.
But Meg I suppose you know
that since both poets died
Breughel's painting's been
cleaned to clear the view
of your unprimrosed path

to Hellmouth. Those stern
watchmen mightn't recognise
Ma Meg the Dulle Griet
unwitched & unbesmirched
washed of muck & murk.

——

After 70 you get
to be a special target.
Medics want a sample
of what they coyly call
by way of welcome to
second childhood your 'poo'.
Then a letter arrives from
Messrs Leasehold Agents
'Our Heads of Terms
enclosed for your approval.'
'Don't sign it'
your solicitor affirms
for a fee equal to next
month's pension. Meanwhile
only your accountant
stands between you & a raid
from the boys at HMRC.
O you mustn't be afraid
you'll be kept abreast
even in the event
of your house arrest
it's for your welfare
& a fond farewell
but in case you foresee
retirement as carefree
afternoons catching up on
Cold War spyduggery
or Digger manifestos
wave them bye-bye.

Bake a cake or
mop the kitchen floor:
housework helps to
keep at bay that pack
of fools on the telly
flashing Union Jacks
in the EU chamber
29th January 2020.

—

Find edges then
increase contrast
test brightness &
saturation by all means —

it's neither what you see
nor what your camera's
witness to whatever
you might have seen

supposing you had
digital vision and
whatever it was would
only show on-screen —

whether fiction's history
or history's fiction's the
hard riddle always posed
& hidden behind scenes.

——

Troops disembarking at Rouen
noted the delivery vans from Fortnum & Mason
a firm you could rely on
to judge what Specialties
the boys at the Front set their hearts on

Lemon Squash Tablets, tin of 12
(Only Fresh Lemon & best Sugar)
Scotch Bun (Keeps for Weeks) about 2lb
Flat tin about 1lb Chocolat Fortmason
1 tin New Season's Roast Grouse, Whole Bird
1 tin Game Patés (Truffled)

Assorted Boxes from 15/- to £5:5:0

or for £1 the Piccadilly Box
By post to France £1:1:4
17 tins including
Turtle Soup Tablets
Peppermint Bon Bons
best Dorset Butter
Oxford Marmalade
Anchovy Paste

probably not for the boys who'd
never sat in a dentist's chair
& arrived at the Front with
a gappy parade of cracked teeth

▷

to gobble bully beef down
& hardtack smashed with a mallet
not quite the delights of jellied eels
black pudding & hotpot they'd had at
home beyond the reach of Fortnum
& Mason in dockland & milltown

On the fifth morning of the fifth week we spotted the
frogs on the paving alongside the smaller pond. They were
probably among the couples splashing about and hanker-
ing to mate the afternoon before. Slumped with faces
pointing away from the water as if paralysed escaping a
home become hellhole. Two were speckled white belly-up,
legs cramped in pain or panic, one female swollen with
spawn. The other two lay flat, heads down and legs dis-
tended, skin red as predicted; one body dissolving into
jelly, puffed and transparent, in a haemorrhaged puddle.
That afternoon we found another, further from the pond
and sheltered between flowerpots. Who when my shovel
touched him tried to drag himself away by his forelegs but
his trunk resisted, too heavy to lift. I smashed his head
with a brick.

Two more on the sixth morning. One swollen belly-up,
the other face down and legs splayed. Motionless all day
but when touched by the shovel late afternoon their legs
stretched and lungs pumped. These frogs are suffering
long slow deaths but in merciful coma. One smash of the
brick isn't always enough.

A crowd of survivors still frolic and mate in the pond but
drop no spawn. Common frogs when breeding often purr
loud as bikers revving up a few streets away. These are
frisky but silent: have they lost their voices?

As its name implies ranavirus mostly attacks frogs but can
also infect toads and newts. It first appeared in England in

▷

the 1980s in the south-east. It has been blamed on the introduction of North American bullfrogs, the immigrant's everlasting doom. It has slowly spread north, perhaps in the wake of milder winters. It is waterborne and has no known antidote. Emptying the pond is a temporary measure but the virus will lie dormant and infect any refill. It usually kills 90% of a colony. Some individuals are genetically immune and will successfully breed, eventually achieving complete repopulation. For some colonies it's wipeout.

Seventh day, one swollen female belly-up. Are pregnant females the prime targets? Should we suppose a virus has like ants and bees a collective mind with supra-personal intentions? The pond anyway awash with mating couples and frantic three- or foursomes, a daylong orgy. Occasional faint purrs answer yesterday's question. We've yet to see the dying crawl from the water. They're probably struck when night's coldest. Most get no further than two feet from the pond. It seems none die without heading for dry land.

Report posted the seventh evening of the fifth week in Europe of coronavirus Covid-19 which may have developed among mammals such as pangolins or bats but as of now seems lethal only to rapacious biggest-brained primates and mostly endangers the older and least fit of the species such as your correspondent mourning those frogs who gladdened his best days.

A logoclast in lockdown
tries to recover that longlost song
'Will yowe walke the woods soe wylde'.
What's he thinking of?
Knocked-out verses & life as
life was in jolly England?
Quickies in the bushes with
one or other siren Boleyn?
The tune's still played
It's only the words that walked out
Only to vanish in a mighty forest.
They'll be as hard to find
these days as a mighty forest
to look for them in. Is the logoclast
imagining some nearby reserve
such as the not so wild Ecclesall Woods?
It would be a comfort to walk there
(the logoclast thinks)
were it not for
(and thinks the subjunctive
is the ideal tense for a lockdown)
a virus not a metonym
for scam or net boast.
Were it not for the posses
armed for moorland vigil
mostly he supposes looking
out for him. Oh him
only scratching down words

▷

he'll only scratch out
when he's done singing
for want of a word
these ticked-off nights
to himself of himself
walking woods soe wylde.

—

riffing with Jack Spicer
under house arrest:

Wherever will I find
an ache or echo or object to
object to as much as to
a stack of obstacles
flaky prophecies I meant
to say flashy prosthetics
voice flagging at half-mask
noises none understand.

Honesty as home decoration
that's moonwort allowing
white shadows wide berth
in the dust left by those
who saw through time.
I'll do as I ought
Refuse until the lights come on

Avenge averagely.
I have a month's supply of sole-
cisms ready to collect
on Dover cliff or if I wish
to skip a few centuries the beach
but there's a storm just now
a swarm of duckbilled platitudes
pesky to contend with.

———

Dr Hellbent on hellebore
paid my dreams a visit
warning me to never
disparage disparity.
I wouldn't call that a vision
'whereout the world
was extraught' but what
you get if you read
Behind the State Capitol
alongside Tom Nashe on
the Terrors of the Night.
What it is to 'confound
in one gallimaufry'.
At 3am Dr Hellbent
listens to the rhythm
of the falling rain
not supposing it's the
Everly Bros' comeback
but Greta Garbo's ghost
crossdressed or just cross.
Pit or pat? Ask Dr H.
Sure as an Easter rose
Doc Hellbent knows.

Lee Harwood had a thing about pangolins
although he told me once he'd only seen
one stuffed in the Brighton museum
he worked in at the time as an attendant.

Whether Marianne Moore met one's unsure.
She said she took some of her description
from 'Pangolins' an article by Robert T. Hart
in *Natural History*, itself a museum piece.
Perhaps she came face to face with one
in the Bronx Zoo but in that case would
she have called it however amusingly
'This near artichoke'? Better that she exalts
the pangolin's part in the 'splendor
which man in all his vileness cannot
set aside'.

       Nowadays & any time
you choose you can watch one on youtube
turning his or her head left & right with
what looks like a smile. He or she's penned
in a Chinese market & up for auction
as either top-price meat or an aphrodisiac
if not the elixir of life. Top-price because
there aren't so many pangolins around in
the 21st century. On youtube because
they're possibly carriers of Covid-19.

Re the problem of constructing a language
in which to send messages to aliens entirely
unlike us & 4+ light years away
Nick Richardson* instances
Ted Chiang's tale about heptapods
'who perceive all time simultaneously'.
As do the Tralfamadorians
or so Billy Pilgrim informed Kurt Vonnegut.
As too did William Blake
which raises the question whether
Blake was an alien — has that
been asked in any message
now heading into outer space?
If so & if an answer comes back
since 4 light years = 24 trillion Earth miles
you & I will never know unless in death
we start perceiving time Blake's way.

* *LRB* 18.6.2020, reviewing *Extraterrestrial Languages* by Daniel
Oberhaus, MIT 2019.

Further to Sir Thomas Browne's notes on bubbles*
such as 'They are more lasting & large in
viscous humidities' & 'Boyling is literally
nothing butt bubbles' & 'Even man is a bubble
if wee take his consideration in his rudiments'
we may pause to reflect that we individual
bubbles when struck by a pandemic are instructed
to associate with no more than five other
bubbles in a catchily defined collective bubble.
Further to which we may worry we'll be caught
in Russell's Paradox again if we question whether
a bubble of six bubbles constitutes a set of bubbles
belonging to itself or not. But that's a bubble
this bubble prefers not to bubble up with.

* Mus. Brit. MS. Sloane 1875, ff. 41-44. Wilkins, iv. 441.

16.7.2020

The hole where your friends used to be needs filling somehow. Be my guests at this celebrated artisan restaurant. No I hadn't been told its single room's a factory workshop, dereliction intact. Sorry its one overhead light is so harshly unshaded and we're seated far apart at its only table, round and formidably spacious. And yes I'm keeping watch on the manager orbiting behind us, tall and glowering viciously down at our shoulders slumped over plates of salmonella.

If I'd only known but apologies anyway. Milord manager snaps fingers to summon the floorshow. The four of them to match the four of us. They sashay through the door I suppose hides the kitchen. Burlesques disguised by brown plastic helmets resembling helium balloons with printed smily mouths not exactly come-hither. All spraycanned HELLO in white paint where their eyes should be.

You mustn't think I expected we'd be noshing crap grub in a cathouse. Let's do a runner. Through the door to what might have been the kitchen but there's no food cooking and nowhere a stove. On the far wall another door guarded by a line of grim matrons, arms crossed firmly as mouths tight shut. But follow me, I'll push past.

Out to a fire escape swaying high above the factory yard and its relics. Steps rusted paper-thin but blame my vertigo, don't the rest of you panic. We'll be back in a tick and yes here we are again at our monstrous round table. Balloonheads still cavorting. I'll pay and we'll be off. Ninety quid ninety quid more than it was worth but cheap at the price if we can go home now. If only. The manager's still on the prowl, round and round us he circles, punching fist into palm. Eat up.

last last words from the message parlour:

Pages ripped from a notebook next day —
it's never what more but what less to say.
+
What you needed to know about tanks
was that some were male & some female.
Males were armed with six-pounders,
females machine guns. This was long ago
in the 20th century, during the Great War.
These days some tanks are transgender.
+
That list you keep of our misdemeanours
is a health-risk. It so enrages you, neighbour,
that you take revenge on a hanging basket.
We pray you'll die soon if not before
although you've rage enough to bore
a way out of a lead-lined casket.
+
It won't matter to the homeless
but a warning to posterity:
the East Devon Tories' Tramps Ball
was another victim of austerity.
+
Granted that commonplace violence
is both cause & effect of common parlance
it follows that louts who are aped
by politicians will ape the politicians.
+
Outside Waitrose a woman screaming
I don't want to be Me. Ever. Ever. Ever.
Just try telling her that anyone from
an uncertain point of view's Anonym.

\+
This uncivil era (earache) of rivals' saliva.
\+
Forlorn as foreknown fireworks
forborne before noon. After midnight
from over there also true to form
in Nether Edge two gunshots.
\+
An outcry's an inquiry as soon as
the scapegoat's snared in the snakepit.
\+
Perhaps the Middle Ages
really were middle-aged:
wouldn't that help diagnose
the 21st century's dementia?
\+
Between ourselves and as
safeguard against relapse
without moving our lips:
us haunt to back come words.

———

riffing with César Vallejo
one Thursday in quarantine:

If you were here we might break out
invalided or since it's only a matter of
where stress falls in-
                            valid. You'd find us
here together caught on both counts
both sized up amiss by those seizing
the chance to take neither side of any
point they choose at any moment
to seem to make. What geometricians.
As if there were sides from which
we might break out. Even if we were
allowed to say that again —
                            if if if &
so on to infinity — if you were here.

riffing with Ted Berrigan
Just think of all the places
you ever yearn to visit
such as once upon a time NYC
names still on the maps but
it's the time you want e.g.
one wet February evening become
morning in the Lower East Side 1963
when things were happy to happen.
There were moments too in Hay-on-Wye
nights pubs opened as
evening became morning & book
deals were struck on sticky tables
but don't go there now expecting
a big green day scouting for box-
fuls of NYC mimeo editions
20 quid if you'll take the lot
in '76 or '80 or even '82
which was about the time the supply
line failed. I can't believe
I really said quote yearn unquote
it's not my sort of word but perhaps
that final quote n unquote
meaning unknown
having popped an extra strong pill
jumped on next or was it last year's back.

———

Dear Laura
locked down
far away
in Richmond, CA.

I knew a man who had a method.
He owned a book by a poet we'll call P
published by a press we'll call X.
He then bought all of P's books
& all books published by X.
Then he bought all the books of the poets
published by X so that he now
owned a lot of books published by many presses
& written by many poets all of whose books
he'd now buy along with all the books
all those presses published
which was a lot in some cases
& so he would go on
until he owned more poetry books than
anyone could read in a lifetime not
exceeding common expectation.
But that man I knew had a method.
After four or more years
he sent all the lots & lots of his poetry books
to sell in job lots at an auction.
He called for a van
& from his point of view
in a manner of speaking
all that poetry vanished.

I doubt it proved a wise investment
but at least he could start again
collecting by the same method
anything he chose except poetry books.

———

riffing with Tom Raworth's
Moving August 28th 2020
when nothing much has moved
hereabouts for 5 months

(the government's been moved
to explain the situation
although we're not told where
the government's moved to)

((cf. the blank entered 10.59pm
June 5th 1970 which could be today
when 'word' recorded at 10.26
would be a word too many))

(concluding note on absence)

In one last photo I've noticed missing among others from my late mother's collection she posed as so many must pose to be snapped beneath the more than lifesize statue of Eric Morecambe waving hands and kicking legs on the promenade at of course Morecambe. I took half a dozen shots before I caught my mother in a fit of giggles as if Eric Morecambe had just cracked the joke of all jokes. This was back in the last days of the reflex camera and it seems I gave my late mother my one print which she framed to sit on the sideboard in her Burgess Hill flat so sunny that this and other photos such as the last I took of my mother and by then cancerthin father laughing together in the happy relief of a blowy afternoon when they could stand for a minute or two alongside the obelisk on Ditchling Beacon were bleached out. That distressed and by now distressing print survives in my mother's collection but I can frame the snap of her encounter with Eric Morecambe only in my mind's eye and probably enhanced.

———

'Could we bring back mammoths
to fight climate change?' asks the BBC.
Exactly who We are is left to float
in the ether which probably belongs
by now to an unnamed party. But
read on & you'll discover that only
last week a churlish thief stole
the world's biggest rabbit so what
hope can there be for the welfare
of herds of resurrected mammoths?

Ah reader, pause & reflect. The BBC
on the same page reappraises Our
beloved Prince Consort recognised
at last as a bigger critter than you or
I could possibly conceive but for
all his exceeding all us titch rabbits
with his might & majesty lately extinct
& so by implication our best hope
dashed of fighting climate change.

———

Best offer on the box set
of your life from Day One
until midnight tonight when
the offer will expire.

Will you take it? And if not
then what? Perhaps you'd
better offer to buy the whole
lot but how can you be

sure one won't get away
to be snaffled on ebay?
Retrieving what's left of
your memory could cost you

more than even you thought
it worth. O it's a scam to make
you ask yourself who you are.
Or is it. Three minutes to go

you'd better make up your mind
how much you mind. How much
in any case did you make up in
the first place & who'll remind you

now you're boxed into a corner.
Remember mephistopheles.com?
At your service. Calling time
kindly but it's time to pay up.

———

He kept bad company in later years.
Hung out with Martial. Rifled Shakespeare's
bawdy. In low comedy revelled,
considering shit the symbol of his era
& truth a compendium of error.
He never quite settled but rarely travelled.
Sat by his window & slowly unravelled.

——

watch how they do
the shortfall shuffle
wingless as a wineglass
at tipping point although
it's no use looking for
respite in semblance
when only things that
can be touched
can be vouched for

(bankers
falling off
their perks,
as if)

var.

(not to set aside questions
raised by misplaced letters
when claiming expenses
on a spreadsheet laid out
like a patient etherised etc
if text test & tabs stab
if either dither among new–
found typos of ambiguity
how will I understand
how well I understand)

▷

medallions of modality
pugnacious poignancies
moving out of tearshot
of honeymoon hotels
for otiose homonyms
Narcissus narcosis
a kind of attitude sickness
also known as
Responsibility Control
doing us some
serious imagery
with focused obscurity
conqueros
withdrawls
Puritantrums
repercautions neither
bidden nor forbidden
'wrecked havoc'

var.

an end to austerity
such as one
sugared augury
after another
           Oyez Oyez Oyez
try tripping out on
simultaneous stimulants
or remember Rita Hayworth
stripping off her glove &
play the beam on memes, boys

var.

buoyant as a buyout clause
succour for punishment
but please no applause —
prehistory's a comfort
in the light so to speak
of more recent events
Fast Radio Bursts
maybe neutron stars embracing
or a magnetar enacting
a solo danse macabre
if not broadcasts
bouncing home to tell us
in around 12 years
rats & pigeons will
inherit the Earth
they've been meek long enough
& as for me my other's
out on parallel parole

correction: 'patrol'

Nether Edge
2009–2021

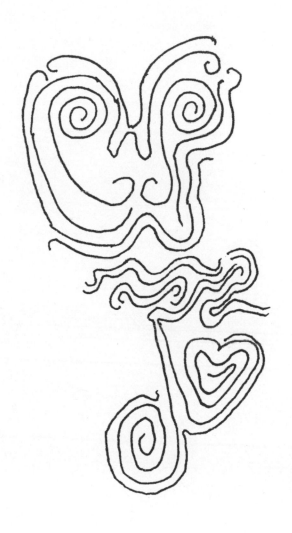

Alan Halsey titles
published by Five Seasons

In Sight of Carnllidi
Hereford Poems Six: 1979

Song of the Rowan
Hereford Poems Seven: 1980

Another Loop In Our Days
two editions: 1980

A Small Yacht Launched with Instructions to the Reader
broadside: 1983

Auto Dada Café
two editions: 1987

The Text of Shelley's Death
two editions: 1995

Marginalien
with graphics CD: 2005

Lives of the Poets
2009

After Sappho frag. 16
broadside: 2015

AS ILLUSTRATOR

Rowlstone Haiku
Frances Horovitz & Roger Garfitt: 1982

O Mother Gaia
Gary Snyder broadside: 1984

Bone from a Stag's Heart
Paul Merchant (cover): 1988

Le Fanu's Ghost
Gavin Selerie: 2006

Hariot Double
Gavin Selerie: 2016

POEMS AND DRAWINGS
The Kilpeck Anthology: 1981